Young Men Talking
Voices from Belfast

Ken Harland

A YouthAction (Northern Ireland)/Working With Men Publication

First published 1997
by Youth Action and Working With Men
320 Commercial Way, London SE15 1QN

© 1997 Youth Action (Northern Ireland) and Working With Men

Layout, Design and Printing by
RAP, 201 Spotland Road, Rochdale OL12 7AF

ISBN: 1 900468 01 8

20027106

Ken Harland has worked as a youth and community worker in Belfast for the past 12 years. Since graduating from the University of Ulster in 1989, he has worked in both the voluntary and statutory sectors of Northern Ireland's youth provision.

A major focus of his practice has included developing work with boys and young men in different settings and providing training in boys work for various youth organisations and staff teams throughout Northern Ireland. He has had several articles published in relation to working with young men, and has been involved in developing young men's health programmes. For the past few years, he has worked in an advisory capacity/consultancy capacity for several youth projects addressing men's issues.

In 1995, he began studying for a Master of Philosophy Degree, focusing on the role of full time male youth workers currently working in Belfast, and exploring the way in which their practice, and their interpretations of masculinity, affect the future development of boys and young men.

Contents

Acknowledgements

There are several people I would like to thank who have made this publication possible. Firstly, and most importantly, I would like to thank the 25 young men who agreed to being interviewed on tape. Their openness, honesty and willingness to discuss different aspects of their lives with myself, albeit often in a 'confined space', made the process both fascinating and enjoyable.

I would also like to thank Youth Action and The Health Promotion Agency (Northern Ireland) for giving me the opportunity to carry out this needs assessment with young men, particularly as this was an innovative area in young men's development.

A special thank you to Trefor Lloyd, who was my consultant throughout the process and who provided me with ongoing and valuable support, direction and advice.

I would also like to thank those youth workers who helped me make initial contact with some of the young men.

Finally, a big thanks to my wife Libby, who has always encouraged and supported me.

Ken Harland
Belfast, December 1996.

Preface

A history of work with young people in Northern Ireland has been the story of young men. We built their characters, encouraged self-discipline, celebrated their prowess on the sports field, encouraged endeavour, provided challenges and, more recently, sought their personal development and participation. Yet, throughout all this, workers and/or volunteers have always had that uneasy feeling that the provision was about distraction and deflection from the streets. The streets were violent places - ritual and random violence on streets of a contested society where young males provided the cannon fodder.

We watched powerless as de-industrialisation and market forces brought a cruel equality as young Protestant men joined their Catholic "brothers" on the dole queue or the dead end training scheme. We were challenged during the 1970s', when work with girls and young women was discovered, new energies released, new language used - 'consciousness raising', 'self-esteem', 'feelings', 'equality' and 'the sexist male'.

We worked away, conscious that, for many young men in working class communities, their traditional routes to manhood were narrowing and closing. We witnessed the changing roles, the brutalisation of many within a generation and yet somehow we did not hear their voices.

As male workers, we saw the birth of the 'new' man, held the new-born baby, shared our feelings, explored our masculinity and felt better about ourselves as men - professionally sussed, committed to gender equality, but frozen when it came to addressing the needs of our young men.

Ken Harland has taken time to listen and, by doing this, has given all of us a privileged insight into the lives of young males from areas of Belfast which have borne the brunt of violence and neglect. Within this generation, there are still the aspiring rock stars, football heroes, cool young men trying to be themselves. While there may be opportunities there for some, for many there is only frustration and unmet hopes.

Beyond the banter and the bravado, we hear their powerlessness, their frustrations, and sense of betrayal by the many adults in their lives. We sense their sadness, their lack of being heard, their struggle to cope in environments which cannot be controlled. Yet we also hear their desires, their hopes, their longing to make things different for their future families. Ken's work is long overdue and brings forward voices that have been ignored for too long.

Denis Palmer
Youth Action (NI).

Introduction:
asking, listening and responding

In 1995/96, a Young Men's Health Project developed out of a partnership between Youth Action (N.Ireland) and The Health Promotion Agency (N.Ireland) which aimed to address recent concerns surrounding young men's health and develop health-related social education with groups of young men. Both organisations recognised the need to develop new ways of working with young men within the youth services which in the past have tended to focus on recreational needs or on young men's aggressive and anti-social behaviour. Their view was that:

"Little work has been done in developing more positive approaches which are concerned with young men's physical, emotional and mental well-being. There is a clear need to develop new approaches for young adolescent males through which they can address the complexities of being young and moving into manhood. Young men need support to allow them to explore the nature of relationships. They need information and advice in relation to health issues, and they need opportunities through which they can learn to share their feelings and emotions about what it is like to be young and male." [1]

An integral aspect of the project was that a needs assessment should be carried out in order to discover, and listen to, what young men considered their needs to be. This would enable workers to reflect upon the setting in which they work, and help them begin to identify skills they may need to develop future work. It was asserted that an understanding of the links between young men, risk taking and masculinity must be central to any strategic intervention into young men's health.

This booklet records the findings of the needs assessment carried out with 25 young men aged 14-16 years between October 1995 and February 1996 (two months before the end of the IRA ceasefire). The young men interviewed were from both Protestant and Catholic backgrounds, living in South and West Belfast. Whilst some were youth club users, others were not. Several of the young men had only recently been released from a young offenders centre. The aim of these interviews was to discuss with young men their thoughts on school, expectations of work, being a man, how they dealt with their feelings, who gave them support and their relationships with their fathers. It was hoped that this process would help identify the needs of the young men as perceived by themselves, and begin to explore possible ways in which youth provision might respond.

The purpose of this booklet is simply to highlight the need to listen to boys - the things they have to say, their thoughts, feelings, ideas, perspectives, aspirations and visions. Perhaps it could be argued that there is no need to listen to boys - that boys say too much already, that they are dominant, forceful, aggressive in their communication, and therefore do not need further opportunities to present their views. Whilst in some respects this may be true, it is nevertheless this perception of young males which often inhibits and restricts them from disclosing their true feelings and beliefs and locks them into typical (stereotypical) male behaviour, whereby their inner thoughts are kept private and excluded from the public arena. To express these inner thoughts is for young men, as it is for all of us men, to make themselves appear vulnerable, weak, not together - in a word, unmanly.

Although we live in a male-dominated society, it is also true that we know very little about men. Until recently, studies surrounding men and masculinity have been absent from mainstream educational research. However, whilst it cannot be denied that there is a developing theoretical approach to men's studies, it must also be acknowledged that society still places real pressures on young males to be strong, mature, capable, sexually experienced, in control, etc. The consequences for boys to act in different ways can be catastrophic in terms of their identity and status amongst their peers. Yet it is evident that many young men do not feel together and therefore must discover alternative ways to cope in order to survive. Although this can be true for all young men, it is particularly evident in working class, inner city areas where there are often high levels of educational under-achievement by boys and where traditional routes to acquiring male status, such as through employment, are less attainable. Consequently, young men are more inclined to prove their manhood through high levels of risk-taking and deviant behaviour; certainly not by speaking openly about emotions and feelings, which many young men regard as feminine qualities and therefore not to be adopted.

The implications of this are colossal for those of us who attempt to respond to young men's needs, as often they do not articulate their needs effectively. This may also be reinforced because the way in which we work with young men is often dictated by how we, as adults, have identified their needs.

Undoubtedly, one reason for this is because young males do not speak openly about their needs, but perhaps a more fundamental reason is that we, as those resourcing young men, do not ask them! If we don't take time to ask young men about themselves, what they think and feel, their hopes, needs, vision, etc, then it is obvious that we cannot be listening to the things they have to say, nor be able to respond effectively to their identified and real needs. The bulk of this book contains many of the views, thoughts and opinions of the young men, in their own words, covering various themes which emerged from these interviews.

Young Men Talking: school

I spoke to the young men about their thoughts on how they learn and the ways in which they are taught. Some were very straightforward about their performance at school, and many were obviously struggling:

Q: How much do you think school has taught you?

"Not a lot, it's just like, the teachers have no time for you, so ya just mess about. I couldn't be bothered then and I got suspended and threw out of school for two days. I didn't go back, and, after a couple of months, I went to a different school." (age 14)

"School has taught me hardly anything 'cause I never really do much at school. I never went much 'cause I didn't like it, but I wish I had of stuck at it better and tried my best, but I couldn't be bothered - I really wish I had learned to spell, I tried to catch up, like, but I couldn't do it." (16)

Some had a real sense of hopelessness:

"I was never good at school, so I didn't really learn. Ya feel wick when everything goes over yer head, like. But, if ya tell them ya don't understand, they just keep going on with the subjects and ya just fall further behind. It makes ya feel really shit, like, 'cause school's supposed to be the place where ya learn." (14)

Several young men blamed themselves for not learning:

"Not much, I'm a messer." (14)

Q: How does school respond to you when you mess?
"*Detention.*" *(14)*

Q: How do you feel when you get detention?
"*Gutted, but all my mates are messers, we all get detention.*"
(14)

Some felt they had learned at school, but still struggled to see the benefits:

"*School has taught me quite a lot - it helps you learn things, but I don't know what things I will need for the future, so it's hard to say if school prepares you well - you only know later in life.*" *(16)*

Others failed to see any benefits:

"*School puts my head away, so it does - it's boring, so it is - a pain in the arse. There's a few things I like - games and P.E. - but all ya do is the same things over and over. I'm not learning anything anyhow, like - well, not much.*" *(14)*

"*I don't like school 'cause they give ya P5 work - spellings and all - but I'm not fussed like, I know how to spell, so I don't say anything.*" *(14)*

"*Nah, I don't like school 'cause I haven't really learned anything - especially the last two years 'cause there's a load of messers in my class and everyone just goes along. If one does it, we all do it. It's mad, like, at times.*" *(15)*

Q: Can you think of other reasons school has not taught you much?

"'*Cause the work yer doing, like, you were doing it in second year - you do it again in third year. It's boring, you lose interest. They think we're not learning enough so they go over the same work. The teachers think we're stupid, or something,* and give up on ya. I'm starting my tests this week and I haven't a clue about them - they ask questions and I haven't the answers." (14)

Not everyone blamed themselves or their peers for not learning at school:

Q: What do you feel you would have needed in the past to help you do better now?

"Better teaching." (16)

Q: What way would you like to have been taught?

"Taught better than I'm being taught - a smaller class of 15 or 16 with a teacher who listens to ya, as well as you listening to him. I'd rather do drugs or something than R.E. you should be able to talk to yer mates without getting detention, like - and not treated like children." (16)

Some were more critical of the school environment:

"Not sitting in a classroom with boards and all; somewhere more comfortable where you can sit down and talk, more than write or whatever - discuss things and watch TV an awful lot more, instead of just copying notes of sheets - ya should have debates or watch videos, instead of just listening to a teacher." (15)

Tensions and frustrations between teachers and pupils were very apparent:

"In school, I just get suspended or detention 'cause, like - well, they just throw books at me and tell me to hurry up, instead of showing you what to do or help ya in any way." (15)

Q: What about your behaviour in school at the moment?

"Well, it's got a bit better, but teachers keep shouting at me, so

17

I shout back and that gets me into trouble, and then all the teachers are against ya. But, ya see, I go to a special teacher, it's something about behaviour, but it doesn't work cause she only does relaxation and all that there, but it doesn't make sense, but I've no choice - I have to go." (15)

Others lacked motivation:

"What's the point of behaving well, 'cause ya see, we're not doing GCSE's, and I think I'm smart enough to do them - but we're not allowed 'cause I'm in one of those classes who probably didn't do my work in primary school cause I got into trouble in primary school, so they think I'm not good enough to do them." (14)

Several young men felt it was difficult to remove labels that had been applied to them in the past:

"They always see me as a troublemaker 'cause I got into trouble once, but they should find out who does the things and look at it more carefully, 'cause they always think it's me, and it's not." (14)

"If you were a messer in 1st or 2nd year, then they would still think yer a messer in 5th form." (16)

"When I was a kid, I messed around and got into trouble, but I don't mess about as much now - but if there is any trouble in the class, they blame me, like . I just tell them I didn't do it, and then I crack up and lose the head." (16)

Some identified their peers as the source of their trouble:

Q: Do your classmates mess about?

"Aye, all the time, and they mess the teachers about a lot." (14)

18

Q: Does this effect you in school?

"Sometimes, like, if they're sitting beside me, they would get me to do it. There's peer pressure, ya know, they peer pressure ya into doing it. But I won't do it - but it effects ya, yer work. It's not the same for girls. Boys are, like, they're into more drugs and stuff, like, than girls are." (14)

Q: Why do you think that is so?

"I don't know." (14)

Q: Have you any regrets about the things you did in school?

"Yeah, this all wouldn't be happening with the police and all only for the friends I got stuck with. They're all troublemakers, and I went along (pause) like a fool." (15)

Others were clearly struggling, both with the environment and the way they were being taught:

"Some of the classes are really f—ing boring, like, you can't take it in. It gets really frustrating. Like, you don't like the subject. You can't take in one and then it just gets dead frustrating and boring - I just want to get out." (15)

Q: When you say boring, do you think most of your classmates think its boring too?

"Yeah, the ones I'm in, like, you know, the classes, most of them, some of the teachers just can't teach. It's the way they teach and it's just dead hard to take it in ..ya just get pissed off with it all." (15)

On many occasions, young men expressed that what they were being taught was way over their heads:

Q: When you say it's the way they teach, what ways are they teaching you that's hard?

"It's dead confusing - one minute they are on a subject you can take it all in, and then they change to something else, and they go too quick, like, do pages 48, 49, 50, and you can't. Like, it is just flying through all those pages, and you don't take any of them pages in." (15)

Q: Do you think the teachers are aware that you feel that way?

"No." (15)

Although some young men understood why some teachers rushed through subjects, this was clearly not meeting their needs:

Q: So, why do you think he or she is going at that pace?

"Just coming up to the exams, you know, trying to get it all done, they go too fast and they don't even care that ya don't understand - all they want to do is say that they've covered the subject, even if ya haven't a baldy what the f— it was all about." (16)

There were others who also felt this way:

"I don't know a thing about science - that's one of the classes I just can't take in. They teach ya that fast ya can't take it in. They should go slower and explain things better to you." (15)

Many believed that their performance in school was directly related to the way in which they were taught:

Q: What is it about school you don't like?

"Teachers. They're slabbers. They don't teach ya nothing. They make you work too hard." (16)

Q: Do you not like working too hard?

"I don't mind working, but they just over-react to everything, and that bugs me." (16)

Some spoke of how they deal with confrontation:

Q: What did you do when they over-reacted?

"I just wouldn't go in, like, and they'd send me out letters and tell ye ye'd better do better or else I'll get into trouble - but I just stay away from school - I don't give a shit what they do." (16)

"I'm not scared of them, like, I've told him where to go. They think, just because their teaching ya, that ya have to do what they say; well, I'm not going to take shit from them, and they know that there, so they do, so they just leave me alone." (16)

Some felt that teachers could not relate to them:

"Am, it's just, am, the teachers. They're sort of, like, harsh. It's like, they live up there and, like, we, ah, live in "The Village" they're living in, like, big houses. They come from a different lifestyle. They don't know our problems. We should be asked if we want to do things, and, if you don't want to do it, ye shouldn't have to - we're not wee kids ya know." (15)

Many of the young men expressed difficulties regarding both the way they were being taught and their relationships with teachers:

Q: What is it about school you don't like?

"Teachers, they're all f—ing slobs; even when ya finish yer work, they just give ya more. Teachers should be more polite to ya. They don't teach ya anything, they teach ya nothing." (15)

"Teachers and the work - it's boring." (16)

Q: What is it about the teachers?

"We're in class C and do nothing - the teachers just give ya books. But we just set them on the desks and just sit there, and they don't give a f—; they just think we're thick or something." (16)

Q: Why do you think teachers do that?

"They don't like us, they see us as troublemakers. If we were in class A they would treat us different - 'cause they're in a higher class, they give them more time. They don't understand ya - they think we're wasters." (16)

Several had clear thoughts on how they would like teachers to relate to them:

Q: What way would you like teachers to be?

"Somebody who's dead on and doesn't pick on ya and gives boring lectures and all that there, gives ya good activities to do in class and doesn't make ya work all day." (16)

"Just for the teachers to be dead on and not strict and all." (14)

"To be friendly. Just to teach you what you're gonna need to know, and not to mess you about and all that there." (16)

For some, their relationship with their teacher directly affected their performance:

"It depends on the teacher you get, like; if you don't get on well with the teacher, you'll probably not do so well in a subject as in a subject where you do get on well with the teacher." (14)

"Some teachers are a bit ignorant and all that there. Some teachers have different methods of teaching, and some teachers just can't teach you." (15)

Others deliberately tried to thwart the situation:

"Well, ya see, me and my teacher don't like each other, so I don't do nothing in class and this gets up his ass." (15)

Some young men clearly desired, and needed, a better relationship with their teacher:

"I think teachers should encourage ya more. I've been off a good lot 'cause I was sick, and the teachers wouldn't go back and help me and I fell behind in work - I had to go to other people. They should've photocopied the stuff I missed." (14)

"I'd just like to be able to tell the teacher what I think or feel about some of the things they teach, but nobody listens to ya." (15)

Others commented on choices they made:

"I was sitting in every night doing nine homeworks and everyone else was out enjoying themselves. I didn't like the uniform and having to wear a blazer. I only have to wear a sweater now. I've only to learn one language now, instead of three." (14)

"I was the only one in my area passed the 11+ and I felt like shit cause they all slagged me and all - so I left that school and went to the same school as my mates." (16)

Some young men recognised that there were other factors contributing to their education other than teachers:

"It's not just the teachers. If the pupils were, like, more respectful, had more respect for the teachers, we could be doing better. Some of them just think, like, GCSE's, they're another 2 years away, not to worry till then. Then they're mucking about and we don't get the work done. And then we're punished for that - but if it wasn't for school, you'd be lost." (14)

"I think some people hold ya back when ya want to do well and, like, if ya tell them ya want to do well they just make an eegit out of ya, and so ya just don't try hard and ya fall way behind with the work." (14)

A recurring theme with the young men was their obvious sense of powerlessness to bring about change:

Q: Is there anyone who asks you what you want to do?

"No. Nobody gives a shit about what I want - I've never been asked what I think I need or what I'd like to do." (14)

"Ya'd think that we would be able to tell the teachers what we want to do and what's the best way to be taught - but we're not asked; we're just told what to do, and ya have to do it." (15)

Listening to some young men, it was evident that school did not meet their needs, nor adequately prepare them for life beyond school:

Q: Can you think of anything school could have taught you that it didn't?

"Aye, lots of things, 'cause all ye do is spellings, and there's no point sitting exams, when I'm not going to pass them - they think I'm not smart enough, and they're probably right." (14)

"I don't know what I'll do when I leave school, like, 'cause I've no exams or anything." (15)

Several young men had strong views about what they needed from school in relation to preparing them for work, and many expressed real concerns about a lack of information and choice:

Q: Can you think of better ways school can prepare you for leaving?

"By giving you more work experience, telling you how to go about certain situations. You only get one week's work experience - this isn't enough." (16)

Q: Did you do any work experience in school?

"No ,I never done any of that." (16)

Q: Why was that?

"Just never got to do it." (16)

Q: Were you ever offered it?

"No. I may have been offered it, but it was dead far to travel and I wouldn't have gone to it. It should be somewhere in yer own area." (16)

Some felt that school should be addressing issues around work throughout secondary school:

Q: Do you feel school prepares you for work?

"Well, like, before we started picking our subjects for GCSE's, they could have told us more about jobs, because now some of us have only started to think about what we are going to do and we have already picked all our subjects - but we mightn't have picked the right subjects, and now we can't change - it's too late." (14)

"I want to be a bricklayer - school should help you do that for, say, a week or two, but it doesn't." (16)

There was a clear need for better and longer work preparation:

"School doesn't prepare ya very well, like, 'cause yer only given a week's work experience to sample and it wasn't long enough, and, by the time ya started to get used to it, ya had to

go back to school. *The teachers told ya things about work, but when ya go out it is actually different.*" *(16)*

Some had a clear picture of the type of job they would like to do when they left school, but felt they did not get the support and advice they needed:

Q: Did you do GCSE's at school?

"*Yeah, but I didn't do well. I thought I would have done better 'cause, you see, I was planning to be an electrician, but I couldn't find a way into it.*" *(16)*

Q: Did you know how to go about becoming an electrician?

"*No, that's what I couldn't figure out, you know, how to go about this. I was wondering about who to talk to, or something, but I didn't find out.*" *(16)*

Q: Did school help you in this area?

"*No, I was left to myself.*" *(16)*

Q: Was there anyone you could talk to at this time?

"*No.*" *(16)*

Conclusions

Although most of the young men seemed to understand that school was important and central to the possibilities of them getting work, many believed that school did not adequately prepare them for future employment. Most of the young men I spoke to were struggling at school and openly displayed feelings of frustration and anger at the type of education they were receiving. One alarming aspect of the interviews was the fact that most of the young men were evidently under-achieving at school. It is with these young men that perhaps school could be more effective in providing opportunities for them to experience quality work placements which would give greater insight into the demands and requirements of employment agencies and the type of skills needed to do the work. I believe that focusing more towards work placements would be of greater benefit to both the young men and those whose responsibility it is to teach them. Several of the young men I interviewed identified this as a real need and felt that school had failed them in this area. This is of particular significance when one considers the importance that having a job is to these young men. (What the young men actually said about the importance of work to them is contained in a future section.)

The young men also recognised difficulties they had in terms of certain teaching styles and the ability of classmates to disrupt and stop school being useful to them. Some said that they lacked general confidence within the classroom, and an overwhelming number indicated that they had very little confidence in their ability to change either teaching styles or disruption in the classroom. The interviews also highlighted the importance of teacher/pupil relationships and how this can influence performance.

The fact that many young men felt that the work was too fast and went over their heads' was a particularly worrying aspect of the way that some young men learn. This appeared to be a major reason for conflict within the classroom. Because of this several young men had become completely disillusioned with school and had no apparent desire to learn. Although some young men had ongoing antagonism with teachers, I often felt that it was not the teachers they were rejecting, but the way in which they were being taught, and the appropriateness of the material being used, that left them feeling powerless and frustrated.

Young Men Talking:
health, sex and relationships

Several young men commented about how little they felt school prepared them for more personal issues:

"You don't do much about drugs and all at school. We have got a class and some man came in, but he only taught you for about an hour and he cannot explain everything you need to know about it. I think you should have a class about that there, that should be one of the main subjects." (age 15)

A number of the young men indicated an unhappiness, or dissatisfaction, with the health, relationship and sex education they had received:

"I only learned about health and sex education in the health centre, not at school. School, or somewhere, should teach you about these things. Anything I learned about sex and all I learned from my mates and just finding out for myself, like, but no-one tells you how to do it like - you find out for yerself." (14)

"You get it in religion, so you do. But it doesn't - you go through abortion and all that, so you do. But it doesn't really - it is good, but that there's the only class you get it in and it only goes on for 4 or 5 weeks, so it does." (16)

Some identified other factors that affected the way they learned:

"We've had the odd bit. Just a brief outline, but not how

29

you're gonna live in later life, like, but as long as pupils are going to sit messing and all that there, it's dead hard to learn. Cause someone says like, masturbation, and they all go ha, ha, wank, good laugh. They just go in and have a laugh, and ya don't take it in." (14)

Q: Why do you think they get on like that?

"Just because some teachers are only new and haven't had much experience like that, and so everyone just says that's an easy class and mess about." (14)

Some see the need for trust and confidentiality:

Q: So you are saying that, in sex education, it's very important that a teacher behaves a certain way?

"Well, if other people are going to make an eegit out of you, the ones that are gonna mess, then you would feel a bit uncomfortable. But if you had a class and the teacher was willing to teach it, then it would be all right. The class would have to be where everyone could trust each other and decide it is not going to go outside the classroom, whatever you decide to talk about." (14)

Others criticised the content of the sessions:

"Sex education is wick: they tell ya nothing. Just tells ya what to prepare for, but it doesn't tell ya how to make them. Everyone knows how, like, to make babies, but they just tell ya how to prepare." (15)

There were many contrasting experiences:

"I never got any health or sex education - we did nothing on that." (15)

"Sex education was good, but we only got it once for a couple of weeks, so we did." (14)

Some spoke of future responsibilities and identified several needs:

Q: Do you feel that you need preparation for becoming a parent?

"I think, if yer gonna become a parent, ya need some sort of support." (16)

Q: Is support available for you at the minute?

"I watch my mum and dad with my young sister (laughs) - changing nappies - that's about it and feeding them, but no-one ever really tells you about it." (16)

Q: Who do you think teaches men to do these things?

"Parents and nurseries, we done science and reproduction - that's about it - the life cycle and all." (14)

Several young men saw the need to learn parenting skills:

"We don't get anything about teaching ya how to be a dad and mind children and all - a man does need that 'cause the woman knows - she gets taught to do it in school, but boys don't get that sort of thing." (14)

Q: If there was a class for young men to look at these issues, would you be interested in going?

"Yeah, probably." (14)

"When I'm older, I think the church should teach you - wherever you get married." (14)

"That should be part of what you get taught at school.. like, yer not going to ask for it, but they should just tell you about it anyhow." (16)

Almost all of the young men see themselves getting married and having children in the future:

Q: Do you ever see yourself getting married or having children?

"Aye (laughs), and two or three children." (14)

Although relationships are important to young men, they were not being addressed in school:

Q: Are you taught about relationships in school?

"No, not in school - but they should have learned ya. They think ya know it all, like, but ya don't. I just let on I know, but I never was told about girls and sex and all, so ya just let on ya know everything (laughs)." (14)

"Yeah, ah, what do you mean?" (15)

Q: About sexuality, relationships between boys and girls.

"Yeah, I think so, but not a lot." (16)

Q: Was it good preparation, was it thorough enough?

"No, it wasn't, but yer not gonna say to anyone, 'Hey, I don't know about sex - will you tell me?'" (16)

For most young men, this was an area they wanted to know more about:

"We didn't do anything like that this year, for some reason, but I would like to learn about health and sex education and all, 'cause nobody tells ya about those sort of things." (14)

Some young men felt that perhaps many adults were uncomfortable talking about sex:

"Adults don't talk to ya about sex and relationships and all - I think they're too embarrassed, but ya need to hear about it, like - we did a bit about it in the youth centre and it was good." (15)

Although several young men had some experience of informal sex education, most had not:

Q: How did you find out about sex and relationships?

"Ya hear it on the streets - ya hear people talking at school."
(15)

"You hear about it from yer mates and all, but ya don't really learn about it all - everybody says they know all about it, but they're spoofing - my mates always go on about doing it and they think, 'cause they've a girlfriend, they know it all - I think schools should tell ya more about it, then ya wouldn't have to find out for yerself. It's, like, as if ya shouldn't talk about it, but everybody wants to know about it."(14)

For the young men interviewed, issues surrounding health and what constitutes a healthy lifestyle were not addressed at all in school:

Q: Do you learn about health issues in school?

"None whatsoever; anything I learned was outside - like in a youth club, or something, but even then it isn't really enough."
(15)

"Nah, we didn't do any of that in school." (14)

"What do ya mean, like?" (15)

Some did not see the need - particularly if they did not take drugs:

"Nah, 'cause like there's nothing wrong with my health 'cause I play football and all and I only have a drink at the weekend - I smoke, like, but I don't take drugs." (14)

"Ya don't have to worry too much about yer health when yer young unless yer gonna take drugs or something." (16)

Conclusions

Young men were very positive about opportunities to develop skills and knowledge about health, sex and relationships. Their current experience seems to be very limited, and varied, with a number of the young men suggesting that poor teaching, and other young men disrupting the sessions, interfered with their opportunities to learn. When asked, young men said they were keen for opportunities to learn and discuss these issues, with several proposing that the curriculum should include more aspects of "life" skills and personal issues that affected them. Although there is pressure on young men to be experienced and sexually aware, it would appear that both school and youth provision do not adequately address this subject, nor offer adequate preparation.

Young men appear to learn without really being taught about it. Sex is a good example of this. Many of the young men I interviewed had received little or no sex education to date, and therefore learned about sex, as I did, on the streets. At present, there is no uniform pattern to the teaching of sex education in schools or youth work across Northern Ireland.[2]

This undoubtedly leads to ignorance and places pressure on young men to learn through experimentation - by trial and error!

The inconsistencies of the young men's sex education experience complies with recent research which found that, in Northern Ireland among fifth form pupils (average age 16), almost half of the boys reported that they had not been given classes explaining menstruation or sexually transmitted diseases (apart from AIDS), and almost one in four said they had never had a class on puberty. [3]

This situation must surely be addressed within both formal and informal education programmes as part of the overall curriculum if young men are to develop healthier lifestyles. Is it acceptable that there are such inconsistencies in young men's experience of sex education? Most of the young men I interviewed expressed a real desire to be taught effective and appropriate health and sex education, and, although they had no preference as to where this could be taught, I believe this is an area that youth work can address effectively. Although there are examples of effective practice within some youth initiatives, most of the young men I spoke to had not received health and sex education in any form. The question must therefore be asked, is current youth provision responding effectively to these young men's needs? Unfortunately, from the interviews that I had with these young men, it would appear that the answer is a resounding no!

Young Men Talking: work

The young men were asked to comment on their thoughts about the importance of work:

Q: How important is it for you to work?

"Very important. You need the money for a house, and, if ya have kids and all, you need to supply them with food and clothes and pay electric. It gets ya off the streets and out of the house and keeps ya from being too lazy. You should work from about 8.30 to about 5.00." (age 15)

"Very important, 'cause, if yer in a relationship and all, or married like, yer gonna need the money for yer family." (16)

Q: Have you any fears about not getting work?

"Aye, you would not be able to support yer ma and da 'cause, like, they've eleven kids and my da is on the Bru as well -and if ya get married, ya need a good job to support yer wife." (16)

Work was very important to the young men interviewed, primarily as a means of getting money:

"Work is dead important 'cause, if ya don't get a job, then ya have no money and can't settle down and get a house and set yerself up for life. Ya need a good job - one where ya can get promotion." (15)

"Ya gotta work, like, 'cause I need money to get myself a car, and so I need to earn lots of money 'cause ya need money to do the things ya wanna do in life." (14)

For others, the implications of not having a job went beyond money:

36

"If ya didn't have a job, ya wouldn't have no money and ya wouldn't be able to do things and ya get classed as a troublemaker by the peelers and all. They see ya standing by street corners and ya get yer name down in a book, or get lifted for nothing." (14)

"I think work is very important 'cause, if I'm working, then it means I'll not get into trouble, I'll have places to go and have money in my pocket. When you're bored, you have to find things to do, and this gets you into trouble." (14)

Some associated work with taking responsibility:

"Work is very important, because, like, if ye get married and have kids or something, then ye have to raise a family. Or, say, something like yer girlfriend gets pregnant. If ye have a house, you have to pay for it." (16)

"It gets ya off the streets and out of the house and keeps ya from being too lazy and means that ya can pay yer own way." (14)

"If you don't work, you won't be able to feed yourself and you would just sit in the house bored - you need a job so that yer family can have a holiday and all." (14)

For some, being the family provider was very important:

"Yes, work's dead important because you're gonna have a family and settle down and have kids and all. You're gonna need to support them. You can't go through life without supporting your family." (16)

"It's very important to have a job 'cause, if yer gonna develop relationships and get married and have kids and all, yer gonna need a good job to look after yer family." (16)

Most of the young men, however, were very pessimistic about getting a job:

"If you rake about like me, then it will be hard. 'Cause, when you rake about, then ya don't learn. I probably wouldn't get a job anyway - 'cause there's hardly any jobs anyhow. I don't want to be a hairdresser, or anything, or work in shops. I'm scared in case I leave school and, ah, there's no sixth form, and, if you leave school and don't get a job, you have nowhere to go. I wouldn't go on the Bru', like." (14)

"It's very hard to get a job, even when ya want a job. Like, even if ya do get a job, it's still hard, 'cause when ya leave school yer nobody, like, so ya have to make a name for yerself so people will come to you for work." (15)

Some young men were without any hope:

"Ya've no chance, sure it's a waste anyhow unless ya've got f—in' qualifications, and I'll not get any of those." (14)

Several associated work opportunities directly with behaviour:

"It's important to work, like, it gives ya a chance. If you were in the paramilitaries, like - all them ones haven't got a job and haven't got a career and all." (15)

"Ya need money to get a house and furniture and all, but it'll be very hard for me to get a job 'cause of my behaviour in school and my record with the police. I'd like a second chance - but ya can't get it." (15)

For many of these young men, the prospect of not getting a job when they left school was a major source of anxiety:

"I worry about not getting a job 'cause, at my age, ya start to go out drinking and all, and ya need a job to get money to go out at the weekends, but if yer a raker like me you've no chance of getting a job." (14)

"I don't think I'll get a job 'cause I've been in trouble a whole lot. If I go for a job and they look up my record, they'll not give me a job - they'll give it to someone with qualifications and all." (16)

Some were more aware (and hopeful) of the broader picture:

"It'll probably be hard because, ah, Northern Ireland has the highest unemployment rates in the United Kingdom, but now that the peace process is here, it might help business and make opportunities." (14)

Some made links with work and mental health issues:

"Well, if you don't have a job, then you don't get out. I mean, like, one of the teachers said to us in school, if you don't have a job, you're unemployed; when you get up in the morning, you don't shave 'cause you don't have no job to go to; then, day by day, you don't start to wash, 'cause you have no job to go to, and then you start to go down and down and down. But if you have a job, then it keeps you going all the time." (16)

Others had a more sophisticated view of the world of work:

"It is going to be quite hard to get a job. Our careers guidance teacher's teaching us now that women are going to get more and more and more jobs, and it's going to be them who are going to get the jobs instead of men." (15)

Q: What do you think of that?

"I think it's true, I do - they're more intelligent, so they are, than half the boys. They listen more, so they do, in class. You can tell by the way you play with them at school - ours is an all-boys class and the girls are doing far more intelligent topics than us. They tell us they're doing, like, say, level 8 maths, and we're only doing level 7. They are doing better 'cause they listen more to teachers." (15)

The young men spoke of how they viewed unemployed people:

Q: Do you know any people around your area who are unemployed at the minute?

"Aye." (16)

Q: What do you think of people who are not working?

"You don't really know about them there, you think they should have a job. I think that the people should have tried harder at school, but it's like they didn't." (16)

Q: Are you saying there that you view people who are unemployed as those that did not do well at school?

"Aye, or maybe they did not try, or maybe they just didn't get the opportunity - people think when you don't work you don't give a shit, but maybe they just can't get a job." (16)

For most young men, doing well at school was the key to getting a job:

"Around our way, there's lots of men who don't work and they can't get good jobs because they didn't try hard enough at school. I'm scared in case I don't get a job 'cause, like, I f—ed around too much at school and it will be dead hard for me now - I don't think anyone would give me a job." (15)

"Well, like, ones I know who didn't give a shit at school have no job, and they just end up standing at the bookies and all and then everybody thinks yer a waster and all - but they've f— all else to do and this gets ya into trouble 'cause ya feel wick when all yer mates are working and have money and all and you can't even go for a drink with them - like, a few of my mates got lifted for armed robbery 'cause they hadn't the money to buy things." (16)

Conclusions

Work is very important to these young men: for most, simply because of money and the status a job gives them. For others, it's because it enables them to fulfil their role in the family, or because it stops them getting into trouble. Some young men considered work important because it keeps them off the streets and mentally stable. A number of young men suggested that the lack of work would lead them to crime or to 'slide' into a slovenly and mental abyss.

Parallel to this were their concerns about the possibilities of not getting work. Some were very pessimistic, others thought that - if they worked hard enough at school - they would get work, and a minority thought that - if they worked hard enough at school and "were lucky" - they would get work. It was strikingly clear from talking to these young men that having a job was something they all aspired to and placed immense value upon. For these young men, their notion of being successful in life is closely linked to the successful working man. Nevertheless, the consequences of not getting a job were something the young men had obviously given considerable thought to. For many, this was a primary cause of anxiety.

Schools and youth work agencies have an important role to match young men's expectations and the realities of the work environment. From what these young men have said, too many of them are resigned to a life without work, or have an unrealistic view of the opportunities available to them. This is of particular importance as we live in a society that is changing rapidly from the one in which we adults grew up in, and where employment opportunities for men are being significantly reduced due to a decline in traditional manufacturing industries. New skills and knowledge are now required to facilitate developments in technology. By the late 1990s', it is predicted that, for the first time since the Industrial Revolution, employment opportunities for women will be greater than those of men. Many of these jobs will be temporary or part-time and characterised by low pay, with little or no training. I believe young men need to be better prepared for this transition and the likelihood of a continually changing labour market. In the past, this was not an issue as there were plenty of job opportunities for men and the concept of a job for life made many men feel secure about job prospects. To help prepare young men for these developments is of acute importance, as almost every young man I interviewed considered work as the main route to success and personal fulfilment. Whilst society reinforces perceptions of the successful man in terms of the nature of his employment, and men gain status and are assessed in a similar way, then the future for many of the young men I interviewed is, at best, bleak.

Young Men Talking: being a man

The young men were asked when they thought they would become a man, what it means to be a man, and their thoughts on masculinity.

There was a broad range of views on when a boy becomes a man.

For some it was age:

"At 18 - that's the age when everybody turns into a fully grown man." (age 14)

"18 -21 - that's when you move out of the house and get a job and pay for yer own food. Ya get yer own house, so ya do, and maybe a car. Ya don't have to worry about yerself and ya don't rely so much on yer mum or dad." (14)

"At 18 or 19 - that's when yer mature and ya can't be a messer anymore - ya've gotta live up to yer responsibilities and all." (14)

"At 18, 'cause ya can drink and drive and do stuff ya can't do before yer 18." (14)

For others, it was more than just age:

"You become a man when you are about 18. I'll have left school and got a job - it's hard to say, there's no actual date, like. A man needs a good temperament, like, you know, able to cope. It's not important to be strong, it used to be more, like ah, because of labour, like ah, more jobs used to be labour, building sites and all, but now it is mostly office jobs, but a

man has to be emotionally strong so he can overcome problems in, say, his work. Well, aye, yeah, a weak or shy man wouldn't really get anywhere." (16)

Others had not thought much about it:

"I don't know what makes ya a man, but I think I'm one now." (16)

"I've never thought about it - I don't know, like, but it probably happens when yer able to look after yerself and yer family and all." (15)

"Ya don't really think much about when ya become a man, like, it's as if one day you'll just say I'm a man now." (14)

Some of the young men had a clear understanding of what becoming a man involved:

"Ya don't have to be dead hard to be a man, and ya don't have to go and drink every night just to be a man." (14)

"You become a man when ya don't get into trouble, ya see it's mostly kids that get into trouble. When ya become a man, ya grow out of it, you're more mature and ya don't want everybody to think he is still a kid." (15)

"Ya stop fighting when yer a man and just be normal - like people who live up the Malone Road - good people who don't get into trouble and are peaceful." (14)

For some, being a man meant being responsible and in control:

"When yer a man, ya gotta be calm with drugs and drink - like, if ya get into it, and say yer 17 and have a girlfriend and she gets pregnant - you don't get too much into drugs 'cause there's gonna be a kid there." (14)

"A man should be a good person and able to take care of things himself." (14)

For several, it was no longer depending on others:

"I will be a man when I have my own mind and can make decisions for myself, am like, independent of my parents and other people." (16)

"When I'm married with kids, 'cause then I'll be like my parents and I'll do for my kids what my parents did for me." (15)

Others had thoughts on what doesn't make a man:

"Some people say when ya smoke or drink yer a man, but that's a load of crap 'cause some people smoke when they're seven or eight - I don't know when I'll become a man - probably whenever I'm married and having sex or something." (14)

Some were hesitant when asked if they were looking forward to becoming a man:

"I don't know, like, when I think of all the trouble I've been in I don't know if I want to become a man - I've seen some men, like, who just waste away, like - especially inside - I've been there and know what it's like - when I'm a man, I don't want to end up a waster - I wanna life." (16)

"If yer left alone, you'd be alright, but all ya get is hassle and crap and then ya get into bother because yer fed up with it all. It is better when yer younger." (14)

"Not really, I'd rather stay young and more active and all. I'm not sure of getting a job, or having to join an organisation". (15)

Q: Is there pressure to join an organisation?

"Yeah, people want to, ah, they say 'Do you want to join this and that and all?'. When yer drunk or out with friends and all, you haven't got a clue - you just go 'Ayeeeee, OK and all', and then, if you say nah, they say yer gonna get sorted, like, and it makes ya scared." (14)

Q: Have you any fears about becoming a man?

"I suppose so - yes, you have more responsibility - your kids and your family depend on ye. A man's looked up to by other people - people younger than him." (16)

"Yeah, like, I wouldn't like to be married and have no job - if I'd no job, I'd get grumpy and all and feel dead low about myself 'cause people look down on you." (15)

While some thought physical strength wasn't very important, others did:

"Yeah, it is important to be able to look after yourself, because of so many beatings and all that there, fights and always getting beatings, especially in yer teens." (16)

"Sometimes it is. Say he didn't agree with, like, if he didn't agree with drink and drugs, he would have to be strong to stand against it because of the pressure. Also, ya need to be able to look after yerself in Northern Ireland 'cause there is people if ya walk past them and ya looked at them they wouldn't like it, so they would try and hit ya, so you would have to stand up for yerself." (15)

Many young men spoke of the need to protect themselves as a man:

"It's important for a man to be strong 'cause you've got a life ahead of ya and you don't want, say, if someone comes up to you and beats ya up, or stabs ya and you might die, you've

gotta mind yer back - be strong." (14)

"Yip, its important to be strong 'cause a lot of men start fights and ya have to stand up for yerself. Ya feel really under pressure when ya walk pass a crowd of fellas 'cause yer ascared of them chinning ya." (14)

"If someone mouths or messes you around, then you've gotta sort it out - you've gotta be able to kick their bollocks in - if yer soft, then you get your bollocks kicked in - that's the way it is, like." (16)

Some of the young men achieved status through being able to handle themselves:

"A man's gotta be able to look after himself. My dad's really strong, and that's important 'cause ya haven't gotta chance. If ya can look after yerself, you've a better chance, and people look up to ya." (15)

Q: Do people look up to you?

"Yeah, 'cause like, the paramilitary hands are all f—in wee hoods, and they think they're hard 'cause they've got guns and all that there, but they only think they are, but they are f—in shit, but if ya can handle yerself, then yer alright. People look up to ya, like." (16)

The young men identified other pressures they experience:

Q: How do you feel about paramilitaries in your area?

"They're just wee lads of 14 or 15 - still at school. But, although they're shit, it does stop some people doing things like, am, yer not going to break into houses if they don't want ya to do them, or rob oul dolls and all, but, like, you're not gonna do that unless yer sick. That's one thing, like, they're trying to stop ya doing." (16)

47

Some feared for their lives:

"You've gotta be able to look after yerself if ya don't wanna die, like. It's like this when yer a kid and it's the same when yer a man." (15)

"See, around here there's a lotta crime and violence, and, if ya can't handle yerself, then it's too bad for you - I get threatened a lot, but I can take it - if you were soft, you would get serious hassle - I know 'cause there's some who are shit scared even to walk out of the area." (16)

"Aye, men need to be physically strong cause they've gotta fight in the wars and all - you've gotta be able to protect yer family and look after them - like, if you don't protect yer family, who's gonna do it for ya?" (14)

Others had evidently given considerable thought to the matter:

"A man needs to be tough and able to handle himself - it's how to get respect - I'm gonna join the army." (15)

Not all thought it was important to be physically strong:

"A man needs to be emotionally strong more than physically strong 'cause, like, if ya get married and have kids, ya have to be strong in case one of the kids was sick or something, or in case his wife's mum and dad died, and ya need to be really strong to help yer wife along." (14)

"No, not muscle ways, but strong in the mind and have faith in yourself, 'cause if you don't, like, you could become a drug addict or addicted to alcohol or something like that." (16)

"I don't think it's important for a man to be physically strong, like - some people think because they're hard men, they are better than everyone else, but I think that's crap - ya need to be able to sort things out in the mind 'cause, like, maybe you

think a girl wants fellas who are dead tough, but that's a load of balls - but, like, if I was in a fight, I wouldn't run away, like." (15)

Some young men had obviously given a lot of thought as to what it means to be a man:

"A man's gotta look after his family and all - it's his job to do that, and he needs to be head of the family - just because you can fight, doesn't mean you can run a family, like." (16)

"I don't think a man has to be dead strong or anything, but there's a whole lot of people who think that, because they're hard men, they can do whatever they like. But, for me, being hard doesn't make ya a man, it's in the mind that yer a real man." (16)

Conclusions

Contrasting opinions from the young men highlighted that they have no clear understanding of how the transition from boyhood to manhood is successfully accomplished. Certainly, I do not advocate the initiation rituals of some countries or tribes throughout the world whereby young men are inflicted with physical wounds that signal the advent of manhood. Nor do I suggest that western societies need such brutal entrances into adulthood, but it cannot be denied that at present most young men appear to be in a state of limbo, whereby they feel jammed between proving they are men and no longer children.

Most of the young men I interviewed spoke of the real pressures they face as they develop into adulthood. Some expressed reluctance at the prospect of becoming a man and having to cope with increased responsibility, particularly in regard to family, home and decision-making. For others, there was pressure from paramilitaries and the fear of getting involved in crime, violence, drugs, etc. Many of the young men felt there was pressure on them to be able to deal with potentially harmful situations by being able to take care of themselves through violent methods. For some young men, this gave them status amongst their peers.

Many of the young men held traditional and stereotypical images of masculinity such as the need to be physically strong, although it was evident that some young men considered this was important in order to protect themselves (or their families) from threat, rather than simply to appear macho, or in order to prove their manhood.

There were others who felt that it was more important for a man to be emotionally strong than physically strong, and who did not believe that a man must always appear masculine nor conceal the more caring and affectionate side of his nature.

These young men expressed many strongly held opinions and beliefs about what constitutes a man and the type of man they would like to become. However, throughout the interviews, there were continual subtle references to the pressures that these young men experience in their lives, which undoubtedly raises concerns about the mental health of young males in our society. The young men I interviewed appear to be constantly having to address, and cope with, a whole range of problematic and potentially dangerous situations in their daily lives, as well as the emotional turmoil normally associated with adolescence.

For many of them, this was simply the consequence, and the price, that must be paid in order to become a man! This has major implications for those resourcing young men, in that a deeper understanding of issues surrounding masculinity and risk-taking behaviour amongst young men is essential in order to better appreciate, and respond to, the ways in which young men behave.

Young Men Talking: feelings

Moving into more health-related questions, young men were asked about how they dealt with their feelings. Comments included:

"What would I do if I felt upset? I would keep it to myself a while - if it was getting too bad, I'd talk to somebody." (age 16)

The young men clearly struggled when dealing with feelings of anger and frustration:

"If I was angry, I usually crack up and then regret it later - it's when I'm angry that I've got into trouble in the past - I end up hurting somebody, and then I'm sorry afterwards - like, a while ago, I hit a fella with a bottle, but he was causing me grief - like, what else are ya supposed to do? He asked for it." (16)

"Sometimes, if I get drunk, I fart about a lot, but, if I get angry, I start fights - I hit my girl and I was scundered." (16)

Most of the young men kept their feelings to themselves:

"Sometimes I just feel shit and fed up and don't know what to do - I usually go on my own - I don't like anyone to see me, so I stay in my room." (14)

"I don't do nothing - I never show my feelings to anyone - if I'm sad, I just keep it in or get pissed or just go by myself." (15)

Q: Why do you go by yourself?

"'Cause of the way ya would be treated. Ye'd get messed about and slagged - ye'd never live it down if ya said anything to yer mates or something, 'cause crying is only for kids and all - crying is, like, seen as a weakness. If someone cried, I would laugh at them and go along with it and all. But it would depend if it was something serious, like." (16)

There are, however, times when young men believe it is acceptable to show feelings:

Q: Are there times when it is OK for a man to show his feelings?

"Yeah, if he loses his job or something and, like, he'd go mad; or say, like, his kid was in an accident." (14)

For some, it was only in extreme circumstances that a man could cry:

"Yeah, like, if someone gets killed and you knew them, or they were family or something." (16)

"Aye, like I cried at my grannie's funeral, but not just, like, for personal problems." (15)

Most of the young men found it difficult to cope with deeper feelings of pain and hurt:

Q: Do you find it easy to show feelings?

"No - only if I'm annoyed, but not if I'm sad - when I'm annoyed, everybody knows, but, when I'm hurt about things, nobody knows 'cause I hide it." (15)

"If I get annoyed or something, I always crack up and do things I'm sorry for afterwards - I would kick tables and doors and all, and hit somebody a dig in the bake - but, if I feel hurt, I just keep it in, like, 'cause I don't want anyone to see me." (16)

"I wouldn't wanna show feelings in front of people - none of my mates do. We just have a good laugh together - I've never done that - no way!" (16)

Once again, young men spoke of pressure they felt to behave a certain way:

"Nah! 'Cause, like, when you're hurt, like, ya'd cry, but not if you're out with mates - ya'd feel scundered, like - they'd think you were a fruit. There's no way I'd show feelings; I hide them." (14)

Q: If you felt like crying, what would you do?

"Try not to cry - especially in front of anyone - that would be a bit of a disaster 'cause of the pressure on ya." (14)

"I used to cry, up to 2 years ago. Now I just go out of the way for a while - but I wouldn't cry because it's childish." (14)

Peer influence was evident:

"It's embarrassing, like, if you're with your mates, you need to act hard. They'd say, 'He's crying'. So you need to act hard. But you can show you're emotional to yer girl. There's pressure on ye to not cry with yer mates. People think yer weak if ya cry." (16)

Some had a clear understanding of why they couldn't show their feelings:

"There's no way you show yer feelings, like, unless yer happy or something, like. But I wouldn't let anyone know I'm hurt or anything, like. I'm not gay: only fruits go around showing their feelings and all - only fruits show sloppy feelings - that's what people think, anyhow - especially yer mates." (16)

"If yer a man, they'd call ya a fruit (pauses); maybe ya have

to cry, but ya can't." (14)

Q: What is it about a man crying that makes people think he's homosexual?

"Are you serious? If ya run about crying, everyone would think yer not a man and can't take it - only fruits cry; sure, everybody would call you that and think, 'He's a fruit'." (16)

"Huh. They'll say he's some man 'cause no man cries." (14)

Q: Do you believe that?

"Nope, but I wouldn't cry." (14)

Q: If you see a mate feeling emotional or crying, what would you do?

"You'd just think he's a gern and smack him one!" (16)

"Although ya know what he's going through, you're always sort of standing up, well am, with yer mates and gonna say, 'He's crying!'. Deep inside, ye'd probably feel for him - but yer not gonna show it." (16)

For some, the implications of crying in front of anyone were unthinkable:

Q: Say, for instance, you needed to cry - could you do that in front of anyone?

"Cry? - Ya wouldn't do that." (16)

"If you started crying, everyone would start laughing at ya and make a joke out of it and call ya a cissy." (14)

Most young men were concerned about what others would think of them:

"I wouldn't want to cry in front of anybody. Ya shouldn't be ashamed, like, but I wouldn't like to do it in front of anyone -

especially ma mates - they would feel down about ya and feel different about ya." (16)

"No. I wouldn't want anyone to see me, 'cause ah, they would put ya down, like, and ah, say you were a girl, or, like, as if ya were queer or something." (15)

Q: Would you fear that?
"Yeah, dead right." (14)

Q: Have you ever cried in front of your mates?
"Wise up!" (16)

Q: What is it about a fella crying that makes people laugh at him?
"They think yer a baby and all - Are ya serious? Do ya think it's OK for a fella to walk about crying and showing all his feelings? There's no way!" (16)

Not all felt this way:

"If I needed to cry, I'd cry. I'd feel bad about crying in front of my mates, like, but I wouldn't feel weak or something like that." (16)

"I'm not ascared to show feelings - some boys are, like, but I'm not." (15)

"Yes, it is important for a man to show his feelings - it helps him get it all out and helps it all. I show my feelings to my girlfriend, not anyone else." (14)

"Men aren't any good at showing feelings, but, if I wanted to, I'd cry. I wouldn't care, I wouldn't feel weak." (14)

Most of the young men perceived boys crying totally different from girls:
Q: Do you think it is OK for girls to cry?

"Yip. It's dead easy for them to cry - ya can offend them dead easy." (14)

"Girls always cry and show their feelings and all - and that's alright - everyone just says, 'It's only a girl', and that's OK." (14)

"Yeah, 'cause they show their feelings and emotions more than boys." (14)

For these young men, crying was a sign of weakness - but only if you are male:

Q: Do you think that it is a strength or a weakness to be able to show feelings?

"A strength - strength for girls - weakness for boys (laughs). It sounds wired up, doesn't it?" (16)

"It's OK for girls to cry, but, in a boys' school, boys are always trying to act as if they are big and strong, as if you were a big lad, so ya wouldn't want to cry, like. But, in a girls' school, they, like, talk about different things, and they would be able to cry - but, if a boy cries, they take the mickey out of ya and call ya a fruit." (14)

"Most men can hold their feelings, so they can, but girls find it harder to hold in theirs." (15)

"It's different for girls. I don't think there's as much pressure on them. They don't have the pressure boys have from their mates." (14)

Some believed it was more acceptable for girls to show feelings:

"If my girlfriend is angry, she yells and shouts and all, and that's alright, but, if I'm angry, I usually fight or get into trouble - girls don't get into trouble like boys 'cause they hold their feelings in better than boys." (16)

"Men won't cry in front of women, but women will cry in front of men - that's just the way it is." (14)

Q: Why do you think men must hold their feelings in?

"Don't know, probably 'cause they're stronger emotionally than women." (14)

Q: Do you think you hold feelings back more than girls?

"Aye, if someone blatters ya, ya just walk away. Ya know not to hit 'em back - just hold yer feelings in - if ya cry, they'd say, 'He's just a baby'." (14)

Q: Are girls seen as babies when they cry?

"No - only boys - I don't know why that is." (14)

Others were concerned about not being able to show their feelings and how this would be perceived by others:

"I think it is important for boys to show their feelings 'cause girls are good at showing their feelings. Ya feel left out 'cause ya have to be hard, like, and not show yer feelings." (14)

Conclusions

In terms of young men's health (and particularly their mental health), comments about ways in which young men deal with and express their feelings were quite concerning. On the whole, young men said that they did not think that men should show their feelings, and that men had to be 'emotionally strong' (what this seemed to mean is 'unemotional'). This concurs with recent research[4] and raises concerns about how young men deal with stress and pressure. The young men said that they could not show their feelings to their friends, and many thought to do so was to display weakness and be unmanly.

Many boys and young men refuse to display traditionally perceived feminine traits such as caring, showing feelings, crying, etc, for fear of being considered weak or unmasculine. This is particularly acute with their peers. However, I believe this can disadvantage young men as they grow up in societies where feminine traits are equated with positive mental health, and stereotypical masculine behaviour is equated with negative mental health. Boys and young men learn from a very young age to disassociate from anything remotely feminine. Most of the young men I interviewed considered the ability to withhold feelings as a strength and something to aspire to. Yet there were certain occasions, such as at "yer grannie's funeral", when it is acceptable for a man to show feelings.

I believe that, in order for boys and young men to develop more fulfilled and healthier lifestyles, they must feel free to possess and display both their masculine and feminine traits and see this as part of healthy human development, rather than displaying personal weakness.

The young men I interviewed were more apt to disclose their strengths and conceal what they viewed as their weaknesses. They clearly felt uncomfortable talking about feeling vulnerable or highlighting the fact that they had needs, as if this was a confession of personal inadequacy. Most young men were more at ease talking about courage, bravado and power. This, in itself, is very significant, because it is primarily in this context that adult workers communicate with young men - in environments where young men prove their value by what they can do, rather than by who they are. Once again, this has implications for approaches to working with young men. Opportunities must be created that will encourage young men to speak of the pain and hurt they experience in their lives.

It is also vital that, when young men speak of the way in which they feel, it is no longer seen as weakness, but as part of normal and healthy human development.

Young Men Talking:
relationships with fathers

The young men spoke about the ways in which their fathers dealt with their feelings:

Q: Have you ever seen your father cry?

"Aye, at my mum's funeral." (age 16)

"Nah. I've never seen my dad cry." (15)

"My dad doesn't show his feelings." (14)

Although most of their fathers did not cry in front of their sons, they did openly display feelings of anger and frustration:

"No way, my da doesn't cry - he can take it, like. He'd laugh and all, but he wouldn't cry about how he feels. Are ya gagging? - If he was angry, he'd kick yer f— in, but he wouldn't cry." (14)

"I've never seen my dad cry - I know there's times when he's sad, but I've never seen him cry - he shouts and all and gets dead angry - I don't know, like - maybe he cries when he's on his own." (16)

I spoke to the young men about the time they spent with their fathers:

"I don't spend much time with him, not really, it's mostly girls in my family. Being the oldest, my father looks down on me - but I'm mature enough now to live a sensible life and have conversations with him." (16)

"My da's always working and I hardly see him. I wouldn't work the way he does, but he has to work hard for all of us, like - he tried, ya know, to, ah, provide for us all, and he works dead hard." (16)

"I would have liked to spend more time with my da, but he never really bothered - I don't know why - I think he didn't really have the time." (14)

Again and again, young men told me they spent very little time with their fathers:

"I don't spend hardly any time with my dad, 'cause he's working and all that there, and I'm at school - if I had a problem, I could go to him, but I usually go to my mum - my dad doesn't do nothing with me, like." (14)

"My dad spends a lot of time away - two weeks sometimes - or three days. I feel more towards my mum than my dad." (14)

Some understood reasons for their fathers not spending time with them:

"My dad keeps me working at school and all, keeps me doing my work and do the things I like, although I don't spend much time with him. You see, he's got two jobs and he's out working, he only comes home for about an hour, gets his dinner, gets some sleep and then goes to the bar to work until eleven." (15)

"I get up earlier than him to go to work and, whenever I come back, he doesn't come in till later than me and we just get our dinner, but he's always watching the news and I don't get talking to him. After dinner, I go out, and when I come in, he's in bed. But every year or so, we go on holidays and I'm with him for two weeks." (16)

Most young men expressed a desire to spend more time with their fathers:

Q: Would you like to spend more time with your father?
"Yeah." (14)

"Ya do, like, but it's hard sometimes - we never really did a lot together unless we were going somewhere, and he's hardly gonna start now, like. But he's always there if I need him. But I don't really go to my da about things, like, unless it's money" (laughs). (15)

The young men spoke to me about relationships and feelings between fathers and sons:

Q: Do you think it is easy for a father and son to show each other love and affection?
"No." (16)

Q: Why not?
"I suppose my father's feelings are towards my sisters and he's hardly gonna tell me about them 'cause I'm a boy." (16)

"It's hard, like, ya see I've three sisters and he loves them more than me 'cause they are wee girls and he always seems to stick up for them more than me. 'Cause I'm a wee lad, he thinks I should be able to stick up for myself. But it's alright; I can stick up for myself, so I don't need so much love and affection and all." (16)

Others had reservations about getting close to their fathers:

"Well, you see, it's difficult, like, I got to know my mum better than my dad, sort of, 'cause sometimes my da gets really angry and I wasn't sure what he was going to do, so I only really spoke to my da, and we didn't show feelings, like." (15)

"I've never really thought of it before - but we don't show love in that way, like - I don't go about saying 'I love ya' or anything." (14)

The young men were asked if there were other men who had influenced them:

"No men ever influenced me - my dad has sometimes 'cause he's dead strong and all and looks after the family - but, like, I don't really look up to other men." (14)

"Some sports stars. I would like to be a footballer, but I don't think I'm good enough." (14)

"My uncle 'cause he's always taking me places and all. He's dead on and I get on dead well with him." (16)

Conclusions

Another very interesting ingredient of the interview content was the fact that very few young men spoke of their fathers as role models. For most of the young men, time spent with their fathers was scarce, to say the least, and definitely not experienced by them as quality time. The young men I interviewed gave rational answers as to why their fathers did not spend time with them. This was undoubtedly something they had contemplated at some stage in their lives. It was significant that almost none of the young men had ever seen their fathers display feelings, such as crying, and that any expression of feelings by their fathers was usually in terms of anger and aggression. It is also worth noting that the young men I interviewed found it easier to display anger and frustration, rather than sorrow and pain - just like their fathers.

For boys and young men, there is also confusion surrounding which male role models they can emulate. The fact that fathers do not spend time with their sons must also raise issues about where young males learn to be role models to their own future children and families. Only a few young men identified an adult male they looked up to, such as an uncle or sports star. This is of particular importance if young men's perceptions of being a man are that men can only show feelings when they are angry and that the more caring and loving emotions must be kept within themselves - locked away and out of sight!

Young Men Talking:
sources of support

I asked young men about what they did when they needed support. Some turned to their parents:

"They encourage ya, if you owed money and all, they'd help you get the money. When you are in trouble, you need to get it solved - only my mum and dad can do that." (age 14)

"They're family and they're not going to blab it about. Like, whenever ya tell yer mates, the next thing ya know it's all over the place." (16)

Others were not so sure whom they would turn to:

"Don't know. It would be hard, like. I stay with my auntie sometimes." (14)

Some turned to their mates:

"I talk to my mates. They back ya up, but we don't talk about what's wrong with us, we just run about together, we talk about a couple of things - but not much." (15)

"I wouldn't tell anybody except my best mates 'cause they won't go around telling everybody and they'd try and help me. I trust them 'cause we do lots of things together and they try to understand me and give me support." (16)

But this was not everyone's view:

"I don't go to my mates 'cause ya don't know if they're gonna

take ya seriously or not, or make a joke out of it, or tell everybody - ya don't know if ya can trust yer mates." (14)

Some would talk to their mates under some preconditions:

"You can only talk to your mates if you tell them not to laugh or tell anyone else and totally forget about it after you have sorted it out or whatever." (14)

"If I've a problem, I go to my ma. If I'm in trouble, I'd maybe tell my mates, but I wouldn't want them to tell my family, I wouldn't want them to know. You need to get the problem sorted out, and sometimes I don't know how, like ah, you don't know what to do." (16)

Some felt they could speak to youth workers in certain situations:

Q: Can you talk to youth workers?

"Yeah, but only if it's not too serious, like." (14)

"Sometimes they rake ya about, like, so I don't talk to them about big problems." (14)

"I do talk to youth workers - they're dead on - well, most of them." (15)

Some had gone to youth workers when they were in trouble:

"If ya needed a reference for court, ya can get a youth worker to give ya one - aye, ya can tell some of them about it all." (16)

"I talk to youth workers sometimes, but, like, not about things that make me sad; only, like, if I was in trouble or something - I might speak then to a youth worker - it depends how bad it is." (14)

Q: What is it about youth workers that makes you go to them for support?

"Like, they don't think bad of ya and they listen to yer problems." (16)

Others felt there was no-one they could turn to for support:

"There's nobody I'd talk to - who'd listen anyhow? Sometimes ya do things that you wouldn't tell anyone about." (14)

"There's no-one I would talk to. What's the point of telling them anything when they won't help ya anyway?" (15)

A few recognised the need for support:

"When I get into trouble, all I want is for it to be sorted out, but you don't know what to do - you've just gotta sort it out yerself - there should be something there to help you." (16)

"I need someone to help me when I'm into trouble or need support, someone to listen, but there's no-one I do talk to - I just go on my own." (15)

Q: How do you feel when no-one will help you?

"It doesn't get me down, like - I can take it." (16)

"It doesn't bother me. Like, say you had a girlfriend and you loved her, and she dumped you, and say you went to your mates for support, they'd just laugh at you and get on like wee kids, so I just keep things to myself." (15)

Most young men had little or no knowledge of support services available to them:

Q: If you were to get into trouble, are you aware of any places you can go to for help?

"No." (16)

"There's a phoneline or something for kids and all, but I don't know of any place you can go to, like - is there somewhere?" (15)

Some were unsure of the consequences of asking for support:

"It's difficult to tell anyone. Say, like, I did something bad or something. I don't tell anyone. Like, who can ya go to - ya just have to deal with it yerself, ya know what I mean?" (15)

"I don't talk to anyone - no way. You see, I try to stay out of trouble now - you see, I know what it's like to be in trouble - so I stay clear of it. If it's something small, I'd maybe tell my mates - but, like, they don't help ya - so, like, there's no point talking to them uns, there's nothing they can do, so I just keep it all inside." (15)

For some, getting support meant having to trust others:

"Ya can't trust anybody in case they slabber it about, like. Then you get into bigger trouble. Yer better sorting it out yerself 'cause, if ya don't, then you could get into worse trouble." (16)

Q: How can things be worse?

"Huh, well, if the boys found out, they'd sort you - so ya have to watch who you talk to." (16)

Although some young men acknowledged they needed support, they did not know where to look for it, or how to ask for it:

Q: What sort of support do you feel you need?

"I don't really know, but there's times when I need to get things sorted out and there's no-one I can go to. I'm ascared of telling anybody in case it gets out and I get into more trouble - anyway, who's gonna want to listen to my problems?" (16)

Conclusions

The fact that the young men interviewed did not seek support is a particularly disturbing area in young men's development. Time and time again I was told, "I just go to my room - I don't know anyone I can go to - I'm not aware of any services where you can get support - I can cope on my own...".

None of the young men I interviewed knew about agencies that they could go to for help, leaving some of them unable to talk to friends and family and unaware of outside services that are claiming to resource them. The only exception to this worrying picture was parents, whom young men did say they would go to. However, recent research[5] has also suggested that there are some personal issues (particularly sex), where parents do not talk to young men and young men do not ask.

Offering support to young men as they develop is crucial and clearly identified by those I interviewed as important. However, having access to support networks, or information on how to obtain support was certainly not part of the experience of the young males that I spoke to. The fact that young men do not seek, nor believe they get offered, support, can mean two things; firstly, as those resourcing them, we believe that we are offering young men support - but clearly not effectively; or simply, we do not offer young men support. I appreciate that, in order to receive support, you must ask for it. However, listening to these young men suggests they feel that, even when they see the need for support, they cannot ask for it, nor know how to ask for it.

This is an area that future youth provision must address. There is a need to develop approaches to our work which includes practical ways of offering young men support. In order for this to be effective, boys and young men must be encouraged to seek support. Undoubtedly, addressing the difficulties and uncertainties young men experience is no easy task, but it is one that must be embraced. The skills of workers are central to ensuring this occurs. This means establishing effective relationships with young men that build trust, understanding, confidentiality, empathy, etc. If we can encourage young males to believe it is not only OK, but normal, for them to seek support, then perhaps they can begin to talk more openly about the pain and difficulties they experience in their daily lives.

One possible constraint to achieving this could be the fact that we, as adult workers, may possess many preconceptions about young men, perhaps stemming from memories of our own childhood, which obstruct us from asking the right questions and consequently restrict young men from talking or seeking help. If our view of young men is that they are competitive, aggressive, macho, without feelings, etc, then it is also possible that we believe that young males do not have the capacity to disclose personal feelings, emotions, aspirations, dreams, vision, hopes, etc. Practitioners must therefore be aware of the way in which their perceptions of masculinity can influence the way in which they work with young men.

Young Men Talking: male roles

The young men had clear thoughts on the roles they would be expected to fulfil in life. Most considered it the man's responsibility to be head of the house:

Q: Whose responsibility do you think it is to bring in money to the house?

"The man's the head of the house, and he's the one who should be working and all - it's OK for a woman to work, but it's the man who should earn the money." (age 15)

"It's up to the man of the house to provide; he's the one who has to do it - like, my da says I've gotta get a job and bring in money to the house when I get married and all, 'cause he thinks it's dead important for a man to look after his family, and I think that's right, so I do." (15)

For some, there were reasons why they could not fulfil their role:

"In our house, nobody brings in any money 'cause my dad's no job, and we just live on the dole." (14)

Q: Do you think it is important for a man to be head of the household?

"Yeah, say something happens, the man takes responsibility and takes care of it all." (14)

Most differentiated between the roles carried out between men and women:

"It's a woman's job to look after the house and the man should earn the bread. That's the way it is in our house, and that's the way I want it to be - It's OK for a woman to have a job, like, but she's gotta look after the kids and all, if there is any - but it's up to the man to bring in the money and be the head of the family and all, if ya know what I mean." (14)

"Yip, 'cause like, he earns the money and the women cleans the house better. They clean and cook and everything." (15)

Q: Do you see that as a woman's job?

"Yip. A man earns the money and the woman cleans the house." (14)

"A man's gotta look after himself and his wife and kids and he's to take care of them 'cause it's his job to do that; if ya don't do that, then everyone thinks yer not a good man." (14)

Some had strong views:

"Women look up to men 'cause they're the head of the house, like. Ya wouldn't want yer wife feeding ya - ya'd feel wick - I wouldn't want that 'cause I'd feel like a failure and people would say, 'He doesn't even look after his family'." (14)

Not all felt this way:

"No, 'cause women do have power and they could control it, like." (14)

"Things should be done equally, 'cause ah, like, it's up to both of them to do it, 'cause you need both to work to have a home and all." (15)

"It should be equal, like, but it's not - the man's gotta do it, or ya feel yer letting yer family down - I would, anyhow. If my wife was looking after me, I'd feel crap." (16)

The young men also had clear thoughts on whose role it was to look after children:

Q: Whose responsibility is it to look after the children?

"The girl's - she knows how to better than boys." (14)

"Huh, my ma's, she looks after all of us, so she does - ya wouldn't want a man doing it 'cause he'd probably drop the baby (laughs). Only joking - nah, but seriously, women are far better than men at looking after kids and all - everybody knows that." (14)

"That's a woman's job to do that 'cause they're better than men at doing it - men get drunk and all, and don't really know how to mind kids - they can do it, like - but not as good as women." (14)

Q: Have you ever been taught to change a nappy?

"No." (14)

Q: Where do you think men learn these skills?

"I don't know, probably when they were a kid, or something, their mum had a baby. My mum's got a wee baby, but I don't like changing nappies and I haven't done it." (15)

Some showed an interest in learning parenting skills:

"Yeah, I would like to learn about that 'cause I'll probably have kids someday." (16)

"I've never really thought of that before, but I think men should be taught how to look after kids, like - 'cause ya see more men looking after babies now." (16)

Others were not so enthusiastic:

"Not really, 'cause I know most of it. Changing nappies looks easy." (14)

"I don't know, like, ya'd feel wick learning that there." (15)

Q: Why would you feel wick?

"'Cause, like, men don't learn them things - it's women who are better minding the kids." (15)

Q: Who do you think teaches a woman to look after children?

"They just know, like - their mums just show them when they're young so they can do it when they've children." (14)

Conclusions

Most of the young men had a clear and well-developed understanding of the roles they would like to fulfil throughout their life and differentiated articulately between what they perceived as male and female roles. Almost everyone said they believed it was their responsibility to provide for their family, and indeed, for many, the idea of their wife or partner fulfilling the role of provider was totally unacceptable. Once more, this highlights the importance having a secure job is to these young men. Yet, because many of these young men believe that the chances of them getting such a job are remote, this again raises serious questions about their mental health.

Although several young men were aware of changes in society in terms of equal employment opportunities between men and women, most believed that it was the female's role to look after the family and clean the house. Whilst some young men felt they would like to learn parenting skills, many felt that this was a role that women were naturally better at performing than men. These comments reveal that young men's attitudes towards the roles they hope to fulfil in life have changed

75

little over the past few years. This would appear to suggest that many of the traditional roles carried out by men in the past are not only aspired to by young men in today's society, but where most young men still expect to gain their identity and status.

Young Men Talking:
areas, spare time and the future

The young men spoke of the areas in which they live:

Q: Is there anything you would like to see in your area?

"Nah, not really, like, but it's just like, at nights, ya get pissed off sitting at the street corners and all - ya get hassle from the cops and then some people tell ya to move or you'll get yer bollocks kicked in and all, so we just go and sit somewhere with a carryout." (age 15)

"Aye, no joy riding and the peace. I'd just like to see peace in Northern Ireland." (16)

Q: Why do you want to see the peace continue?

"Since the ceasefires, it has been brilliant - before it was crap - you weren't able to go into town without yer mum or dad." (15)

Q: Do you feel you can go anywhere in Northern Ireland now?

"Yes - except into a Protestant area." (15)

Q: If there is a ceasefire, why do you feel you cannot go there?

"'Cause, if yer going in and they heard you were a mick, they would chase ya, and when they got ya - they would just kill ya." (15)

Q: What things do you do in your spare time?

"Go to the bandhall, do a leader's course in the youth club, get blocked and walk the streets - there's nothing else to do." (16)

"All I do is sit at the street corner - there's nothing else to do, especially later at night when everywhere's shut." (15)

Drugs and alcohol played a key role in young men's spare time:

"Get pissed when I can afford it." (16)

"I try not to get into bother, like, 'cause ya have to watch what ya say and where ya go. So I don't do too much, like, just go to the club, or hang about the streets, or sip a few cans." (15)

"Watch videos, get drunk and take the odd bit of dope and hopefully get laid (laughs). Sounds like a good night's crack, doesn't it?" (16)

I asked the young men what they expected to do in the future:

Q: Do you ever see yourself getting married?

"Aye, well, I'd like to do that. When yer young, that's something to look forward to. It's just, like, ya want yer own wee family. Like, my mum and dad had a wee family, and that's the way I want to be when I grow up - have my own family, my own home and children." (16)

"Yeah, and have children as well (laughs loudly)." (14)

Q: Why do you feel that is important?

"'Cause you want to have responsibilities, and all that there, when you grow up. You don't want to be someone with no life - having a family gives you a purpose in life." (14)

"What's most important in life is to have a job, get married and have kids." (14)

"All I need is a good job, a wife and family, and a good social life - everybody does this." (14)

Most young men spoke of getting married, having a family and a job to support them:

"In the future, I'd like a good job and get married and have kids. I'm pissed off getting f—ed around and being bored - I like living in Belfast, but I'm a bit scundered with paramilitaries and the troubles and all - I just want to do ordinary things - just get a girlfriend and settle down." (15)

"I'd like a good home and a good job, and to have a wife and family and be healthy." (14)

Others had concerns about the future:

"I want a place of my own, but I'm too young, so I am. I don't want to end up homeless and have no job 'cause there's a whole lot of people like that. I know ones who have no job and nowhere to live, and I don't want to end up like that." (15)

"I'd like peace in Northern Ireland, so I would, 'cause I would like someday to have kids of my own, and I don't want them to see the killings and murders and all that I've seen. The troubles here have ruined this country, and you have to be careful all the time. Before the ceasefire, it wasn't safe to go where you wanted, and it still isn't safe and you get pissed off with it all." (16)

Conclusions

Most of the young men appeared optimistic about their futures, although it was evident that they had concerns about lack of employment opportunities. The young men spoke positively of their family relationships, which may account for so many of them hoping to meet a girlfriend and perhaps get married and have a family of their own. However, the uncertainty about being able to afford or acquire 'affordable' housing made some young men question whether or not they would be able to provide adequate accommodation if they had a wife and children.

The IRA ceasefire ended two months after these interviews took place. The political conflict in Northern Ireland was a major source of concern for the young men in terms of their personal safety and future lives. Most of them worried about leaving their own area for fear of being identified as a 'Taig' or a 'Prod' and getting a beating. Paramilitary organisations and their members appear to have a strong negative influence in the daily lives of these young men. This is a factor which, either directly or indirectly, affects each of the young men, and there is a major source of resentment at being 'ordered' as to how to behave in their own communities.

Asking, listening, responding:
the worker's role

The interview material reveals some very interesting comments, some of which will be familiar and others less so. Nevertheless, the interviews as a whole reflect something very unusual - young men talking about themselves and their lives. What appears to be equally unusual is how rarely young men are asked about their lives. During the process of the interviews, I became increasingly aware of the importance of listening to young men and what they have to say. On occasions anger was displayed - particularly when the young men felt powerless, helpless and without hope. However, for me the most surprising and satisfying aspect of the interviews was the fact that most of the young men were very eager and able to talk, and did talk openly and honestly when they were asked. Although, at times, they struggled to articulate this effectively, they nevertheless seized the opportunity to talk and be listened to. Contrary to my initial concerns, there was a desire by the young men to voice their views. Young men often report how rarely teachers, parents, and even youth workers, ask them what they feel and think - we must provide them with opportunities to talk.

To create appropriate environments for young men to reflect on their lives, and for them to have outlets - particularly for the strain between their expectations and the realities of their future lives - is very important for young men's mental health. Because young males do not frequently talk openly about their views of the world, the factors that impact on their lives, the pain and hurts they feel and experience, the ways in which they cope, and what they need to help them address their problems, these often become the silent aspects of their lives. Perhaps the main reason for this is because young men are not asked about how they feel and what they think. From the young men's comments, they find the seeking of help very difficult, and therefore any initiatives taken by workers and agencies servicing young males will be of enormous value.

Whilst these interviews were carried out with only a small number of individuals, it nevertheless provided 25 young men with an opportunity to reflect and think about being a man and how this relates to masculinity, risk-taking and health issues. Perhaps more importantly, the interviews also provided an opportunity for young men simply to speak and share their views on certain aspects of being young and male in the mid 1990's. The challenge is therefore not only to find ways of enabling young men to talk, but also for us, as those claiming to resource young men, to listen.

In being prepared to take the time to listen, we must begin not only to appreciate the things young men have to say, but also to consider how best we can develop effective ways to respond. Not that this is an easy task. Youth workers, for instance, often report difficulties in moving young men away from the sport and activity curriculum. They also report difficulties in maintaining discussions with young men, and a reluctance in young men to talk about themselves. What this short series of interviews has revealed, however, is that, when given the opportunity, young men will share their thoughts and feelings, and are more than capable of talking and communicating at a deep and rational level about themselves and their needs.

Gender understandings and expectations

Often, young men's attempts to discuss fears and feelings takes the form of banter. Whilst humour is always an effective way of communicating, young men often use inappropriate and aggressive banter to relate to each other, which places immense pressure on them to be able to take a slagging in order to prove they are one of the boys. It is this type of behaviour that can make young men sense they dare not talk about how they truly feel, and conform by responding to others in the same manner.

Unfortunately, male gender roles force boys to reject as feminine a wide range of characteristics that are simply human, such as the experience and expression of their emotions and feelings, e.g. fear, helplessness and vulnerability. The suppression and rejection of these emotions leaves boys and young men isolated from others and reluctant to talk about the way they truly feel. The fact that young men feel they cannot, indeed dare not, show their feelings was a recurring theme throughout the interviews.

While 25 semi-structured interviews do not make a MORI poll, some of the comments tell us important things about young men's lives and how we as workers might respond to them. Overall, the thoughts and concerns of the young men interviewed were surprisingly similar, although they came from different cultural backgrounds and traditions. In many ways, their needs, fears and aspirations differ little from those of most adult men - the need to get a good job, have friendships, relationships, get married and perhaps someday have children. However, there is also the conflicting challenge of realising these aspirations and having their needs met whilst living in areas of Belfast where unemployment is among the highest in Britain, and affordable housing is difficult to obtain. For these young men, there is also the poignant reality of having grown up in a society which has been beleaguered with political violence and division throughout most of their lives. Even at a time of so-called peace, many of these young men feared for their lives outside of their own area.

One of the most worrying aspects of the interviews was the extent to which the young men receive support in coping with difficult situations and circumstances and dealing with hurt and pain. In most cases, only special friends were trusted enough to share personal fears and anxieties. Even when the young men did share with close friends, it was only at a certain level, and without disclosing deeper hurts that were likely to expose vulnerabilities or be perceived as personal weakness. Some felt they could talk to their parents, in particular their mothers. However, the majority of young men said they spoke to no-one, nor knew of any support or services that were available to them. I believe the interviews pose some serious questions for those of us who work with young men and the organisations which claim to resource them.

Powerlessness and worthlessness

The purpose of this booklet has been to highlight the fact that, if boys and young men are asked questions, then they will have important things to say. The interviews also highlighted the pressure young men feel they are under to act in a particular way, irrespective of what they themselves think and feel, and their feelings of powerlessness to change either the way their friends respond to them, the way in which teachers teach them, or the life opportunities being offered to them. It was in this context that most of the young men felt anger and frustration.

Traditional work with young men has focused on their health through the provision of activity and sport. However, whilst this has consistently attracted and involved young men, it has also tended to leave the more thinking and reflective aspects of the health curriculum, at best, to chance. Statistics reflecting young men's health continually show how young men jeopardise their health by unnecessary risk-taking, through behaviour such as not wearing a seat belt, drunkenness, criminal and sexual activities and eating snacks.

Many young people in our society grow up coping with feelings of worthlessness, hopelessness and a lack of value - recent figures show 42% of deaths for young men were as a result of accidents, with a further 25% from suicide and undetermined injuries[5]. Whilst drug problems and high levels of unemployment impact on the lives of young people, depression is a major risk factor for suicide. This undoubtedly has implications for future approaches to men's work, as young men are the least likely group in the population to use mainstream health services[6].

(It was acutely apparent that many of the young men I spoke to were benefiting little from formal education provision and the various programmes aimed at facilitating the transition from school to work. Because of this, many young people are effectively dropping out of mainstream education and training and are in real danger of becoming marginalised and alienated within society. This view is supported by recent research into the profile of young people aged 16 and 17 who are not in education, training or employment and henceforth termed

'Status 0'[7]. These findings reveal that young people who are in 'Status 0', particularly for long periods of time, tend to become demotivated and discouraged with respect to their chances of success in the labour market. Economic research[8] has also shown that those who experience unemployment as young people are significantly more likely to experience unemployment as adults).

Effective work with young men must facilitate expression of their opinions, thoughts, feelings, expectations, etc, as well as attempt to free young men from the need to continually prove themselves to others. Young men have a fundamental right to be heard, and this includes listening to their pain, hurts, hopes, aspirations and vision. If young men are encouraged to talk about the pain they experience in their lives, I believe this will contribute to healthier lifestyles and enhanced mental health in the development of young males.

Worker role modelling

Adult males working with young men have a real opportunity to play a major role in their development, and, by presenting young men with consistent examples of behaviour, can become effective as role models in their lives. Not that workers can take the place of fathers, but the uniqueness of their roles and relationships with young men provides many opportunities for positive and healthy role modelling.

One way to achieve this is for us, as workers, to set consistent standards of practice. Perhaps, if we can begin to disclose our feelings in an open and appropriate way, then this in itself will show the young men we work with that possessing feelings and emotions, and being able to communicate this effectively, is central to human development. However, the difficulty with this is that, for many of us who work with boys and young men, we too may not have been given the opportunity to talk about our pain and hurts, and therefore do not deem it necessary to encourage young males to talk openly about theirs. If we, as adults, have become masters at suppressing our feelings, emotions and the struggles we wrestle with about our masculinity, sexuality and identity, then perhaps we will also find it difficult to talk to young men at this level. We, too, may have discovered ways to hide our fears, and learned to exist by proving our manhood through a series of stereotypical behaviours. This is because to speak of our feelings and emotions is to expose our own vulnerability and therefore risk displaying weakness. However, the suppression of feelings and emotions, such as pain, fear, hurt, anger, etc, that young men experience in their lives, can be damaging and detrimental to their future development, and therefore opportunities must be created which will encourage young men to talk about what they think and feel. This must be a fundamental requirement of all approaches to work with boys and young men.

Traditionally, much of the work male workers carry out with boys and young men focuses on keeping them out of trouble, reducing disruptive behaviour, anti-sexist work, etc. This often means that work begins with a negative focus, and is therefore not a sound basis on which to encourage human growth and development.

Because of this, I believe there is a need to assess how effective we are as workers in listening to young males, and to begin to question why they are not talking about the real issues and needs in their lives. Training for workers in this area is essential if they are to find effective ways of enabling boys and young men to become more comfortable and intimate about talking about themselves and identifying needs.

Breaking the male mould

Although the initial goal of the interviews was to carry out a needs assessment among young males, during the interviews I became strikingly aware of how little time is actually spent listening to what young men have to say. This is because much of the work with young men is often reactive, rather than pro-active, or based on identified need. Whilst spontaneous approaches must always be a feature of effective work with young men, more effective strategies must be developed to meet their needs.

Carrying out this series of interviews affected me profoundly as I listened to the pain, struggles and reality of the lives of these young men. I was amazed at the consistency and commonality of their thoughts and feelings on themes such as how they learn, what they want from life, how they interpreted their own specific needs, their fears, their thoughts on becoming a man, what constitutes a healthy lifestyle, etc.

One significant aspect emerging from the interviews was the fact that the young men were totally unaware of the impact that their comments had upon myself. To them, it was normal, to be expected, part of becoming a man. For me, it highlighted the fact that we need to examine seriously the way in which we work with, and communicate to, young men. For those of us providing a service to young men, in the light of my own experience and the content of these interviews, I believe there is a need to question and examine whether or not we are really meeting the needs of boys and young men, or are we part of a system which perpetually reinforces negative, unhealthy and unattainable images of what it means to be a man?

Recommendations

The recommendations that emanate from this series of interviews are as follows:

1   If young men consider school as the major preparation for work and getting a job, schools need to provide more effective, and longer, work placements. This is of particular importance for young men who are under-achieving academically.

2   There needs to be opportunities within schools for young people to influence their own learning and to voice their thoughts and opinions in terms of the materials used in classes and the environments in which they learn.

3   There needs to be a more uniform and consistent approach to health, sex and relationship education between schools and youth provision, in order that young people receive the same standard of learning.

4   Health, sex and relationship education needs to be incorporated within school and youth service curricula.

5   The curricula need to include more aspects of "life skills" and personal issues that affect young men, both now and in the future.

6   Gender work with both girls and boys needs to be incorporated within school and youth service curricula.

7   Approaches to health, sex and relationship education need to include offering parenting skills for young men.

8   As gaining employment is of great importance to young men, more advice and information about realistic work options needs to be available to them. Schools and youth agencies have an important role to match young men's expectations and the realities of the work environment.

9   Because young men do not actively seek help, they need better access and more effective information in regard to support networks and resources available to them.

10 Further research needs to be carried out into the way in which young men seek support and the effectiveness of agencies which claim to resource them.

11 Approaches to work with young men need to be flexible and enable spontaneous, as well as strategic, responses to meeting needs.

12 Work with young men needs to include an assessment stage where workers are supported to discuss needs with young men, reflect on the setting they work in, the skills they may require to develop, and the overall outcomes of the project.

13 Approaches to working with young men need to include providing opportunities for young males to talk about their feelings and the pain they experience in their lives. This needs to be viewed as both normal and necessary for healthy human development and growth.

14 Those working with young men need to appreciate the importance of listening to what young men have to say.

15 Those working with young men need to have an understanding of issues affecting young men's lives, their mental health, and an appreciation of links between health, masculinity and risk-taking behaviour.

16 Practitioners need to be aware of how their own perceptions of masculinity can influence their practice.

17 Training needs to be made available for workers to increase knowledge on issues surrounding masculinity and innovative ways of communicating more effectively with young men.

18 Further research needs to be carried out into the mental health of young men.

19 Individuals and agencies working with young men need to record, monitor and evaluate the work in order that others may benefit and learn from their experience. This will contribute to the identification of what good practice might be, and how practitioners, and those resourcing young men, can work towards the delivery of quality youth work.

20 Funding bodies need to provide financial assistance for research into young men's health, and for initiatives aiming to develop new, and innovative approaches to working with young men.

References

(1)   Lloyd, Trefor. **Young Men's Health - A Youth Work Concern** (1996): *Youth Action & Health Promotion Agency (N.Ireland)*.

(2)   **Sex Education in N. Ireland Schools - Views from Parents and Schools** (1996): *Health Promotion Agency (N.Ireland)*.

(3)   **The Health Behaviour of School Children in N.Ireland** (1994): *Health Promotion Agency (N. Ireland)*.

(4)   Young Men failing to seek help in **'Young People Now'** (February, 1996); and **Suicide in Young Men - A Prevention Strategy for Dorset** (1996).

(5)   Aggleton, P. **Young Men Speak Out** (1995): *Health Education Authority, London*.

(6)   Suicide Reduction - Developing a Strategy in **'Working with Men'** (1996:2).

(7)   Armstrong, D. Young People on the Margin in Northern Ireland in **'Labour Market Bulletin 10'** (1996): *Training and Employment Agency*.

(8)   Narendranathan, W. & Elias, P. Influences of Past History on the Incidence of Youth Employment: Empirical Findings for the U.K. in **'Oxford Bulletin of Economics and Statistics 55 (2)'** (1993).

Appendix

Methodology & Learning

Whilst it was essential to provide young men with an opportunity to express their needs, it was also vital that an effective method of gathering the information was used.

In order to achieve this, Youth Action and the Health Promotion Agency commissioned Trefor Lloyd, an author and trainer on men's issues, in the role of consultant to myself. This proved to be an invaluable resource to me, as together we moved from the original idea of collecting data into developing a series of interviews that would encourage boys and young men to speak.

We designed a semi-structured questionnaire under specific themes that we hoped would enable young men to speak and not only encourage them to answer preset questions, but also allow the young men freedom to raise their own issues as the interview progressed. It was decided that each interview should last around 20 - 25 minutes and also be taped so that I could focus on the things the young men were saying without the distraction of having to write during the interview. To judge the effectiveness of this approach, I carried out four pilot interviews which clearly revealed to me the qualities needed to be a component interviewer. My first impression of the tapes that I listened to was horrendous, and I soon realised there were many skills I needed to learn - and quickly!

None of the young men I interviewed felt comfortable with the idea of being interviewed and therefore I had to spend some time in advance of the interviews trying to explain exactly what I was trying to do. I think their initial fears were heightened by the fact that the interviews would be taped. Responses from the young men included "What do you want to talk to me for?", "Why are you taping this?", "Who's going to listen to the tapes?", etc - all legitimate questions. I assured the young men of confidentiality and that I was genuinely interested in trying to find out about issues that affected them, their thoughts, feelings, beliefs, etc, in order to attempt to identify ways in which agencies could begin to respond effectively to their needs. This appeared to be satisfactory, as every young male I spoke to agreed to be interviewed - even the ones I'd only met on the day of the interview.

During the initial pilot interviews, I stuck rigidly to the semi-structured questionnaire. This proved to be a serious error as I was restricting the young men's flow of conversation. The content of the interview was determined by the next question, rather than the issues that the young men had identified. By adhering too much to the structure, I was not allowing the young men to speak fluently and say the things they wanted to say. I also found it difficult initially to pick up on the issues being raised by the young men whilst simultaneously focusing on the questionnaire. This method of interviewing was quickly amended, and, in future interviews, I responded to the issues being raised by the young men, rather than those imposed by the questionnaire. As the interviews progressed, there were many occasions during interviewing when the questionnaire was not used, or only used for reference, and the interviews became more conversational and subsequently more effective. Both the young men and myself were much more comfortable with this procedure!

Throughout the interviews, it was evident that the young men struggled initially with the idea of just talking and sharing thoughts with another person. Frequently I was told, "No-one's ever asked me that before," or, "That's the first time I've spoke about anything like that."

It was comments like these that led me to believe that young males are seldom being asked about how they feel or what they think. On occasions when they are asked, I believe many young men have learned how to give the 'right' answers, or the type of answer they think adults want to hear. For many boys and young men, their experience with adults has been primarily one of adults sorting them out, changing their behaviour or condemning their actions. The problem with this is that young men feel adults want to control them, or channel them into a particular type of behaviour. Therefore, their answers and responses to adults are frequently determined by the context in which they find themselves. Because of this, the things young men say may not be what they actually feel, or believe, but mere responses to appease adult concerns or inquiries.

I found that, during the interviews, once the young men realised there was no hidden agenda, and that I was genuinely interested in their views, and that it was okay for them to be who they were without being condemned for it, they spoke freely and openly, disclosing many fascinating, frank and honest beliefs and opinions. The series of interviews often became a deep-levelled discussion, whereby both the young person and myself were very much at ease and fully engaged in open conversation. In attempting to extract information from boys and young men, I found this approach to be appropriate and the key to effective interviewing.

Throughout the interviews, the young men spoke about many aspects of their lives, including sensitive and controversial issues, as well as their perceptions and aspirations for the future. What became increasingly apparent during the interviews was the fact that, the more interest I showed in what the young men were saying, the more they had to say.